William Kelley

The conscription

Speeches of the Hon. W.D. Kelley, of Pennsylvania

William Kelley

The conscription
Speeches of the Hon. W.D. Kelley, of Pennsylvania

ISBN/EAN: 9783337283124

Printed in Europe, USA, Canada, Australia, Japan

Cover: Foto ©Suzi / pixelio.de

More available books at **www.hansebooks.com**

SPEECHES

OF THE

HON. W. D. KELLEY, OF PENNSYLVANIA,

IN

THE HOUSE OF REPRESENTATIVES,

ON

THE CONSCRIPTION;

THE WAY TO ATTAIN AND SECURE PEACE;

AND ON

ARMING THE NEGROES.

WITH A

LETTER FROM SECRETARY CHASE.

PHILADELPHIA:
PRINTED FOR GRATUITOUS DISTRIBUTION.
1863.

THE CONSCRIPTION.

This "Act for enrolling and calling out the national forces" was framed to be more efficient for war purposes than were the existing militia laws, less burdensome upon the treasury and the people, and more humane to the poor, who have the aged, and infirm, and helpless dependent upon their labor for support. These objects, sanctioned by patriotism, economy, justice, and humanity, have been attained as nearly as the unequal lot of mankind will permit. This law, enthusiastically welcomed by the armies of the Republic, referred to by other nations as the highest evidence of the determined purposes of the United States Government, dreaded by armed traitors, and denounced by rebel sympathizers at the North, bears in every section and in every line evidence of the patriotism, justice, and humanity of Congress.

Contrast the provisions of this denounced act with the provisions of the existing militia laws of the United States, and of the militia laws of the several States. By the existing militia laws of the United States, the President is authorized to call into the service of the National Government the militia of the several States. By these laws, and by the laws of the States, certain classes of persons are excepted and exempted from military duty—from being drafted into the service of the United States. These exempts are not the poor, who have widowed mothers, aged and infirm parents, motherless infant children, or fatherless and motherless young brothers and sisters dependent on their labor for support. No, not these! Neither the national laws nor the laws of any State in the Union exempt the poor, who have the aged, the infirm, the

(3)

helpless dependent upon them. At the call of the Government under these laws, they must leave widowed mothers, aged and infirm parents, fatherless and motherless sisters and brothers, and motherless infant children who are dependent on their daily toil for support, and be hastened away to the camp and the battle-field.

Who, then, are exempted by the existing militia laws of the United States, and of the several States of the Union? Not the poor, the dependent sons of toil, but the most fortunate and favored of the people—members of Congress, custom-house officers and clerks, postmasters and clerks, (a host in themselves, whose support comes out of the money of the nation,) professors and students in colleges, and ministers of the gospel, judicial officers and other officials, Quakers, Shakers, and persons who may profess conscientious scruples against bearing arms, members of engine companies, hook and ladder companies, or persons otherwise connected with the fire department. The Conscription Act, on the other hand, exempts, in addition to such as are physically or mentally unfit for military duty—*First*, the Vice-President of the United States, the Judges of the United States Courts, the heads only of the executive departments of the National Government, and the Governors of the several States.

Second. THE ONLY SON LIABLE TO MILITARY DUTY OF A WIDOW DEPENDENT ON HIS LABOR FOR SUPPORT.

Third. THE ONLY SON OF AGED OR INFIRM PARENTS, OR PARENTS DEPENDENT ON HIS LABOR FOR SUPPORT.

Fourth. WHERE THERE ARE TWO OR MORE SONS OF AGED OR INFIRM PARENTS SUBJECT TO DRAFT, THE FATHER, OR IF HE BE DEAD, THE MOTHER, MAY ELECT WHICH SON SHALL BE EXEMPT.

Fifth. THE ONLY BROTHER OF CHILDREN NOT TWELVE YEARS OLD, HAVING NEITHER FATHER NOR MOTHER, AND DEPENDENT UPON HIS LABOR FOR SUPPORT.

Sixth. THE FATHER OF MOTHERLESS CHILDREN UNDER TWELVE YEARS OF AGE, WHO ARE DEPENDENT UPON HIS LABOR FOR SUPPORT.

Seventh. WHERE THERE ARE A FATHER AND SONS IN THE SAME FAMILY AND HOUSEHOLD, AND TWO OF THEM ARE IN THE MILITARY SERVICE OF THE UNITED STATES AS NON-COMMISSIONED OFFICERS, MUSICIANS, OR PRIVATES, THE RESIDUE OF SUCH FAMILY OR HOUSEHOLD, NOT EXCEEDING TWO, SHALL BE EXEMPT.

Eighth. Young men between the ages of eighteen and twenty are exempt, for the reason that experience proves that soldiers under twenty years of age cannot sustain the burdens of camp life as well as men between the ages of twenty and thirty-five.

These exemptions of the Conscription Act (so called) are in favor of those upon whose daily toil the aged, infirm, and helpless rely. Is it, as has been charged upon it, making "infamous distinctions between the rich and the poor," to EXEMPT THE ONLY SONS OF POOR WIDOWS, and to compel members of Congress to fight, procure substitutes, or pay for substitutes? to EXEMPT THE ONLY SONS OF AGED OR INFIRM PARENTS DEPENDENT ON THEM FOR BREAD, and compel the whole army of custom-house officers, postmasters, and Government clerks to fight, procure, or pay for substitutes? to EXEMPT THE ONLY BROTHERS OF FATHERLESS AND MOTHERLESS LITTLE BROTHERS AND SISTERS DEPENDENT UPON THEIR DAILY TOIL FOR SUPPORT? to EXEMPT THE FATHERS OF MOTHERLESS INFANT CHILDREN DEPENDENT UPON THESE FATHERS' DAILY TOIL FOR SUSTENANCE, and compel State judges, justices of the peace, clergymen, and college professors to fight, procure substitutes, or pay for substitutes? Shame on the men who misrepresent the beneficent provisions of an act passed to uphold the cause of our imperiled country !

The 13th section of the act in question provides that any person drafted and notified to appear at the rendezvous, may, on or before the day fixed for his appearance, furnish an acceptable substitute to take his place in the draft; or he may pay to such person as the Secretary of War may authorize to receive it, such sum, not exceeding $300, as the Secretary may determine, for the procuration of such substitute, which

sum shall be fixed at a uniform rate by a general order made
at the time of ordering a draft for any State or Territory.
Any person may furnish an acceptable substitute to take his
place in the draft at any price for which he can procure one.
Every drafted man is at liberty to furnish a substitute at such
rate as he may agree to pay the substitute; or any drafted
man may pay such sum, not exceeding $300, as the Secretary
of War may determine, to procure a substitute.

The sum to be fixed by the Secretary is not to exceed
$300. It may be less, it cannot be more. This provision
was put into the law for the sole and single purpose of KEEP-
ING DOWN THE PRICE OF SUBSTITUTES, so that men of very
moderate means, and poor men, could more readily obtain
substitutes. It enables the Secretary to fix the sum which
will be the price of substitutes. Without this provision, it
was believed that the price for substitutes would go up at
once to $1000 or $2000, so that none but rich men could obtain them. If any drafted man can obtain a substitute for a
sum less than that fixed by the Secretary, he is at liberty to
do so. This authority conferred upon the Secretary to fix
any sum less than $300 was purposely given to check specu-
lations, to keep down the price of substitutes, and it must in-
evitably do so.

Partisan malignity, in its blindness and madness, would pervert a measure framed to protect the very interests of those
who most need protection into a distinction in favor of the
rich and against the poor.

THIS ACT FOR ENROLLING AND CALLING OUT THE NATIONAL
FORCES GIVES ASSURANCE TO THE WORLD THAT IT IS THE UN-
ALTERABLE PURPOSE OF THE NATION TO CRUSH OUT THIS
WICKED REBELLION. Denunciations of its provisions can only
fire the heart and nerve the arms of traitors, thus putting in
peril the holy cause of our country, and the precious blood of
its heroic defenders; and by reviving the waning hopes of the
rebellion, will render more absolutely necessary the putting
into execution the draft provided by the act. The only way
in which it can be averted is by promptly arming the willing

hands of loyal men in the rebel States, and by immediately
yielding a united and enthusiastic support to the Government.
thus speedily and thoroughly crushing the hopes, and effect-
ually baffling the efforts of the rebels.

REMARKS OF HON. WM. D. KELLEY, OF PENNSYLVA-NIA, IN REPLY TO THE OPPONENTS OF THE CON-SCRIPTION BILL.

Delivered in the House of Representatives, February 24, 1863.

Mr. Speaker, the discussion upon this most important bill
draws to a close. The discussion has, it seems to me, been
made the occasion for proving, not the dangerous powers of
the bill, but the necessity for some such provisions as it em-
bodies, whereby every species of "treasonable practice" may
be quickly suppressed.

The gentleman from Kentucky (Mr. MALLORY) inquired this
morning when or in which of our wars such powers had been
asked for. When I ask, in return, was the exercise of such
powers necessary before? Sir, there was little occasion for
their enactment during our earlier wars. When a few influen-
tial men of Pennsylvania during the revolutionary war talked
as gentlemen have talked on this floor, the executive councils
sent them far inland into the then remote State of Virginia.
They were seized, by night or by day, wherever they could be
found, and forthwith hastened upon their journey thither, and
the right to the writ of habeas corpus expressly denied them.
That transaction was approved by George Washington, and
the Continental Congress passed a bill of indemnity, covering
all parties concerned in it. There were it is true cow-boys in
those days in the South, and as this instance shows, a few false
and craven creatures in the North who sympathized with the
enemy and prayed "for peace on any terms," but they were
so few that they dared not hope to be able to debauch the
sentiment of the army, so few as not to hope, as is now hoped
by the disloyal managers of the opposition, to be able to para-
lyze the arm of the Government.

During the late war, the men who attempted to embarrass
the Administration charged with its conduct, were overwhelmed

by public indignation, and the few who attempted to interfere with the morale of the army were given a summary trial under a drum-head court-martial, and executed by order of Andrew Jackson. This action called forth the famous Coffin hand-bill, the enduring infamy of the author of which some gentlemen on the other side appear to emulate. Sir, the right of self-defense inheres in every man and in every government, and the bill under discussion provides surely and wisely for the maintenance and defense of the Government of the United States against traitorous sons in the South and sympathizers with traitors in the North—men working in a common spirit to a common end: those with force upon the battle-field; these with subtle poison that reaches the mind and heart,—with the perverted or invented fact and false conclusion that may seduce from his true fealty the ignorant but enthusiastic citizen and patriot.

The gentleman, in flagrant disregard of the rule of the House, said that no man, no single member, was willing at the beginning of this Congress to stand where THADDEUS STEVENS, ELLIOT, and LOVEJOY now stand. It was on the 7th of January, 1862, that from this seat I prayed that our Administration might be taught speedily to avail itself not only of the resources of the North, but those of the enemy, that it would strike them in the tender point, that it would throw them upon their own resources for a supply of food and clothing, as it was its duty to do, by proclaiming protection to every loyal man and woman that should come to the standard of the country. My language, as I find it in the Globe, was:—"And I pray God that it (the Administration) may so far read the laws of war as to learn that it is the duty of Congress, the generals at the head of the several columns of the army, and the Government of the United States, to cut off all the resources of the rebels now in arms against us. It is the first and last law in war. Its thorough enforcement is called for by all the promptings of patriotism and humanity, and promise internal and external peace to our distracted country."

I have always stood where those gentlemen stand on the question so inopportunely discussed by the gentleman from Kentucky, (Mr. MALLORY.) But, for his own purposes, he would teach the people of the South, and especially of the Border States, that the objects of this war have been perverted, that it is no longer waged for constitutional ends or by legal means. He says truly that the sense of this House was expressed in the resolution of his venerable and distinguished colleague, (Mr. CRITTENDEN,) and adds, that the spirit of that resolution has been abandoned. Sir, while it was hoped and believed that there was some lurking patriotism among the controlling minds of the South, and that they might be influenced by a conciliatory spirit, we were all willing to accept peace and a restoration of the Union as things then were; yes, waiving our right to take advantage of the great wrong that had been committed, and overturn the institution that instigated it, we said to them, "Come back, and all the past, even to this moment, shall be forgotten." How delusive was our hope! What was then is not now. Since then 200,000 of our brave countrymen sleep their last sleep in Southern soil, and over the graves of these murdered Americans I never will shake hands and bow and beg pardon of their murderers; nor will the American people. We cannot have indemnity for the past, but we demand and will have security for the future.

I am for exercising all the rights and powers of the Government in this behalf. I am, as I believe the majority of the House is, for eradicating, wherever it may constitutionally do it, that poison, that subtle poison that engendered this rebellion, which made those graves. The gentleman says that the friends of the Administration no longer march to the music of the Union, that they dance to the music of Greeley, Lovejoy, and Stevens. Said he, "the gentleman from Pennsylvania, the Chairman of the Committee of Ways and Means, had educated them up to his measure." He did my distinguished colleague honor overmuch. The events of this era are under the management of no man or set of men. It is to the music of the spheres that the patriot army and the country march. Providence is the guide. He alone controls the march of events; and the music to which the country moves is the spheral strains which inspire undying faith and dauntless courage in the cause of justice and mercy, and that peace which, resting on these foundations, shall endure forever. Sir, the music to which we march inspires us by recalling the highest glories of the past; its seraphic strains breathe forth the hopes and joys of the bright and illimitable future which is to follow this night of strife and woe.

Not my colleague, but God has been our instructor. He has brought us forward, step by step, until at last we are about to enact a law in which we recognize man as man. Nor is the bill demanded by the philanthropist alone. Eighteen months of providential teachings have so far educated us that the most stupid have learned that four millions of people on our side are better for us than the same four millions warring or working against us.

The bill before us is to stand as law for three years. It is consistent with legislation already on the statute book authorizing the President to arm and equip all able-bodied men, irrespective of color, that may be needed for the suppression of this rebellion, and it must not be emasculated by adopting the amendment of the gentleman from Ohio, [Mr. Cox,] and inserting the word "*white*" before men. Let it stand as it is, and it will give us all the soldiers we need.

Mr. Speaker, let me repeat, that it is God who is teaching this people and their representatives by his mysterious providence. Why, the question is asked, could not this country have progressed peacefully as it was progressing? Why must this war come? Sir, I know not why, but, in the bitterness of a heart, stricken at many points by the loss of friends and kindred, and the greater sorrows of others, as it is upon us, I hail it as the era of a new and higher birth for man and for society. I know not why it is that all great blessings come to us through pain and sorrow. It is to the agonies of the Garden and the Cross that we owe our sublime faith and immortal hopes. Who can tell the anguish and pain that are compensated by the first cherub smile that plays upon the cradled infant's cheek? And why is it that through the pains and lingering torments of the sick-room or the horrors of the battle-field that we pass from cares and sorrow to the better and happier world? I cannot explain God's providence, but I do note its visible fruits, and am taught to behold in the agony of my country the sure presage of a new and higher life for her.

"Pass this bill," exclaims the gentleman, "press onward, press onward, and I will invoke revolution." No, sir, let me not do him injustice; he said, "I will hail revolution." What does he mean? Does he mean to say, from his desk in this House, that if we dare to pass this bill he and his friends will resist it by force? If that be his meaning, I tell him that the sons of Pennsylvania who marched to protect his home, and the homes of other Kentuckians, and who now sleep there in green mounds, have not died in vain, and that their graves are sacred shrines, dear to the heart of the people of Pennsylvania, which they never will consent to visit in a foreign land. Let his hail inaugurate a new attempt at revolution, and the Northern army that has protected him and his will clear the earth of him and them. I deal not in threats, but in this hour of our country's peril it is not for us to be too nicely careful of our language, when we hear from the other side the cry of "peace on any terms," and are told what the people of this or that State will not stand, and finally, that if we do not yield to a despotic minority, they will hail revolution.

The gentleman from New York, [Mr. STEELE,] in the midst of patriotic protestations, echoes the strain, saying we do not want an abolition war, we have supplied all the men we have been asked for. Who does want an abolition war, or wherein does this bill propose to make one?

The gentleman says that he and his friends do not like the way "the machine is being run." I suppose not. Men who denounce every measure by which it is proposed to save the Republic are not likely to approve the manner in which the machine has been run lately.

The Richmond Enquirer agrees with the gentleman and those with whom he labors in the endeavor to poison the popular mind, that "the machine is running in the wrong direction." Let it speak for itself. The coincidence of opinion between the gentleman and it is the more remarkable, as he is a prime patriot and its editor is a first-class traitor.

I read from the Richmond Enquirer of the 10th inst.:—

"THIRD STAGE OF THE WAR.

"We have fairly entered upon the third stage indicated by the President in his message, namely, that of a war for subjugation and extermination. The people of this Confederacy, isolated and shut up from all the world, have now to encounter the most horrible and demoniac effort for the assassination of a whole race that history has yet recorded, or we believe will ever have to record till history grows gray. For it is not every century, it is not every æon, that shows the world a Yankee nation. Yes, the Confederate people have now at last to strip for battle—it is a people that must this time very literally conquer or die.

"No doubt it would be agreeable to believe that this last stage of the war will soon be over, and must end in the speedy destruction of our intended murderers. But look round the map of the Confederacy, and judge if we can soothe ourselves with this belief. In the very heart of the country our gallant sentinel of the Mississippi—heroic little Vicksburg—has sustained, indeed, and baffled two tremendous sieges: but a third time her citizens see pouring in around them from the North and the West enormous masses of the beleaguering foe; iron floating batteries again crowd down upon her; and, even as you read these words, two hundred heavy guns may be thundering upon her defenses, a hundred thousand men may be pressing to the storm of her ramparts. Again

she will drive them off, perhaps, and remain the famous maiden city of
this hemisphere, the bulwark of the West; so be it! But the vision we
see on the Mississippi does not look very like exhaustion or despair on
the part of the foe just yet.

"And again, look to the mouth of the mighty river. New Orleans is
not a maiden city; alas! the base rag that has so often been rent and
trampled before Richmond and before Vicksburg flies from all the towers
of that deflowered city. Hordes of hungry Yankees, armed to the teeth,
sit in the shade of her orange groves, and station negro guards over the
mansions of her noblest citizens. All her best and fairest have to lament
every day that their goodly city had not been laid in ashes before it
became a haunt of obscene creatures. No sign of relaxation there!
And, but a short way off, Mobile, by the shores of her spacious bay,
keeps diligent watch and ward, expecting, in the light of each morning
sun, to see the thrice accursed stars and stripes gleaming through the
smoke of a bombarding squadron. All along the Gulf, and around the
coast of Florida, this omnipresent enemy, who is said to have just been
playing his last card, is shutting up every river and planting his guns on
every strong place. Savannah, shut in from the sea by Fort Pulaski, in
the hands of the same inveterate Yankee, listens for the first boom of the
artillery that is to level her walls with her sandy soil; and Charleston,
grimly calm, but with beating heart, stands waiting the onset of the
great armada.

"Those few acres of old Oyster Point, it seems, already swept and
devastated by conflagrations, are to be the object and the prize of the
most potent armament by far that American waters have ever seen.
This very moment, it may be, the black Monitor batteries are steaming
between Sumter and Moultrie. No signs of relaxation, of discourage-
ment and despair in the enemy here! Pass further, and you will find
the whole coast from Charleston to Norfolk, and every river to the head
of tide-water, and every creek and sound formed by the sea islands,
swarming with their gunboats and transports, ready to pour in masses
of troops wherever there is a chance of plunder, bridge burning, and
general havoc.

"From Norfolk all around by Chesapeake and Potomac, we are guarded
by gunboats, and no living thing (save skulking smugglers) suffered to
enter or go out. On the Rappahannock two hundred thousand men wait
for a drying wind to move 'on to Richmond' once more, led by a genuine
apostle of extermination. At last the savage Abolitionists of Massachusetts have the right man in the right place. Heretofore they have
rather wished the defeat of Lincoln's generals on the Potomac, because
they seemed to be soldiers and not thieves or assassins; but with Hooker
they feel at home; under Hooker they count upon owning Southern
plantations and giving law to Southern vassals. To possess himself of
the property of others, a genuine Yankee will, perhaps, even fight.

"And Northwestern Virginia is desolated by Milroy and his men; and
Kentucky and the half of Tennessee, the richest and fairest lands of all
the West, are entirely in the clutch of the enemy, while the rivers bring
them up fleets of transports; and Rosecrans, with another large army,
threatens to sweep all opposition from his path and join the other brigands
who are crowding upon Vicksburg.

"Where, in all this wide circuit, does the invasion seem to be fainting
or giving ground? All round the border, and in the very heart of the

Confederacy, the foot of the enemy is planted and his felon flag flies; and it means subjugation and extermination. It is, indeed, the third stage of the war, and we believe the last; but the struggle will be desperate. If it be the 'last card,' it is one on which the stake is life or death, honor or shame—either our name and nation will be extinguished in a night of blood and horror, or else a new sovereignty, the newest, fairest, proudest, will take her seat among the powers of the earth, with the applause of man and the blessings of Heaven."

I do not wonder that those who find in the Internal Revenue Bill a mere means of extending the corrupt patronage of the Government, and in the Bank Bill and the bill now before the House only the unconstitutional agencies of unconstitutional and despotic power, should, in view of the Richmond Enquirer's complaints, feel that the machinery of the Government is running a little wrong.

But let me briefly turn to the gentleman from Ohio, [Mr. Cox.]

In the course of the tirade against the Administration and its policy, misrepresenting both, he indulged his sportive mood by quoting an alleged private letter of the dead Douglas. Oh, that Douglas lived to-day, how would he rebuke men who make such speeches and gloss them over with his name! He says there was a letter from Senator Douglas showing that a compromise would have been made had it not been essential to the Republicans to drive certain gentlemen from the Senate, in order to secure the confirmation of certain men whom the President desired to nominate to high offices, such as Schurtz, Clay, etc. Senator Douglas was a truthful man. Let me answer the gentleman from the columns of the Globe, and let the Democratic Senator from California, [Mr. LATHAM,] and the fit successor of the sage and hero of the Hermitage, vindicate history and the buried Senator from their foul aspersion.

The speech of this grand old "pro-consul," as some gentlemen on the other side delight in calling military governors and successful generals, will be found in the 46th volume of the Globe. I quote from page 487. Senator Johnson said:—

"The Senator told us that the adoption of the Clark amendment to the Crittenden resolutions defeated the settlement of the questions of controversy; and that, but for that vote, all could have been peace and prosperity now. We were told that the Clark amendment defeated the Crittenden compromise, and prevented a settlement of the controversy. On this point I will read a portion of the speech of my worthy and talented friend from California, [Mr. LATHAM;] and when I speak of him thus, I do it in no unmeaning sense. I intend that he, not I, shall answer the Senator from Delaware. I know that sometimes, when gentlemen are fixing up their pretty rhetorical flourishes, they do not take time to see all the sharp corners they may encounter. If they can make a readable sentence, and float on in a smooth, easy stream, all goes well, and they are satisfied. As I have said, the Senator from Delaware told us that the Clark amendment was the turning-point in the whole matter; that from it had flowed rebellion, revolution, war, the shooting and imprisonment of people in different States—perhaps he meant to include my own. This was the Pandora's box that has been opened, out of which all the evils that now afflict the land have flown. Thank God, I still have hope that all will yet be saved. My worthy friend from California, [Mr. LATHAM,] during the last session of Congress, made one of the best speeches he ever made. I bought five thousand copies of it for distribution, but I had no constituents to send them to, [laughter;] and they have been lying in your document-room ever since, with the exception of a few, which I thought would do good in some quarters. In the course of that speech upon this very point, he made use of these remarks:—

"'Mr. President, being last winter a careful eye-witness of all that occurred, I soon became satisfied that it was a deliberate, willful design, on the part of some representatives of Southern States, to seize upon the election of Mr. Lincoln merely as an excuse to precipitate this revolution upon the country. One evidence, to my mind, is the fact that South Carolina never sent her Senators here.'

"Then they certainly were not influenced by the Clark amendment.

"'An additional evidence is, that when gentlemen on this floor, by their votes, could have controlled legislation, they refused to cast them for fear that the very propositions submitted to this body might have an influence in changing the opinions of their constituencies. Why, sir, when the resolutions submitted by the Senator from New Hampshire [Mr. Clark] were offered as an amendment to the Crittenden propositions, for the manifest purpose of embarrassing the latter, and the vote taken on the 16th of January, 1861, I ask, what did we see? There were fifty-five Senators at that time upon this floor in person. The Globe of the Second Session, Thirty-sixth Congress, part 1, page 409, shows that upon the call of the yeas and nays immediately preceding the vote on the substituting of Mr. Clark's amendment, there were fifty-five votes cast. I will read the vote from the Globe:—

"'YEAS—Messrs. Anthony, Baker, Bingham, Cameron, Chandler, Clark, Collamer, Dixon, Doolittle, Durkee, Fessenden, Foot, Foster, Grimes, Hale, Harlan, King, Seward, Simmons, Sumner, Ten Eyck, Trumbull, Wade, Wilkinson, and Wilson—25.

"'NAYS—Messrs. Bayard, Benjamin, Bigler, Bragg, Bright, Clingman, Crittenden, Douglas, Fitch, Green, Gwin, Hemphill, Hunter, Iverson, Johnson, of Arkansas, Johnson, of Tennessee, Kennedy, Lane, Latham, Mason, Nicholson, Pearce, Polk, Powell, Pugh, Rice, Saulsbury, Sebastian, Slidell, and Wigfall—30.

"'The vote being taken immediately after on the Clark proposition was as follows:—

"'YEAS—Messrs. Anthony, Baker, Bingham, Cameron, Chandler, Clark, Collamer, Dixon, Doolittle, Durkee, Fessenden, Foot, Foster, Grimes, Hale, Harlan, King, Seward, Simmons, Sumner, Ten Eyck, Trumbull, Wade, Wilkinson, and Wilson—25.

"'NAYS—Messrs. Bayard, Bigler, Bragg, Bright, Clingman, Crittenden, Fitch, Green, Gwin, Hunter, Johnson, of Tennessee, Kennedy, Lane, Latham, Mason, Nicholson, Pearce, Polk, Powell, Pugh, Rice, Saulsbury, and Sebastian—23.

"'Six Senators retained their seats and refused to vote, thus themselves allowing the Clark proposition to supplant the Crittenden resolution by a vote of twenty-five to twenty-three. Mr. Benjamin, of Louisiana; Mr. Hemphill and Mr. Wigfall, of Texas; Mr. Iverson, of Georgia; Mr. Johnson, of Arkansas; and Mr. Slidell, of Louisiana, were in their seats, but refused to cast their votes.'

"I sat right behind Mr. Benjamin, and I am not sure that my worthy friend was not close by, when he refused to vote; and I said to him, 'Mr. Benjamin, why do you not vote? Why not save this proposition, and see if we cannot bring the country to it?' He gave me rather an abrupt answer, and said he would control his own action without consulting me or anybody else. Said I, 'vote, and show yourself an honest man.' As soon as the vote was taken, he and others telegraphed South 'We cannot get any compromise.' Here were six Southern men refusing to vote, when the amendment would have been rejected by four majority if they had voted. Who, then, has brought these evils on the country? Was it Mr. Clark? He was acting out his own policy; but with the help we had from the other side of the Chamber, if all those on this side had been true to the Constitution and faithful to their constituents, and had acted with fidelity to the country, the amendment of the Senator from New Hampshire could have been voted down, the defeat of which, the Senator from Delaware says, would have saved the country. Whose fault was it? Who is responsible for it? I think that is not only getting the nail through, but clinching it on the other side, and the whole staple commodity is taken out of the speech. Who did it? Southern traitors, as was said in the speech of the Senator from California. They did it. They wanted no compromise. They accomplished their object by withholding their votes; and hence the country has been involved in the present difficulty."

Mark you, Mr. Speaker, the men who defeated that compromise in the spirit of falsehood and misrepresentation which engendered this rebellion, and which is here and now trying to sustain it, walked out of the Hall and telegraphed to the people they had infuriated that they could get no compromise.

Sir, this bill is important in another aspect.

There are powers beyond the Atlantic: France is there; England is there; and the passage of this bill will be an announcement to all governments which feel disposed to meddle in our affairs that if they attempt it, they will have an organized nation to meet. We will pass this bill not as a threat; we will pass it because the exigencies of the times require it, and the knowledge that we have passed it will cross the Atlantic in twelve days. Their statesmen will see that they had better keep their fingers out of our pie, lest they may find concealed therein a steel strap with sudden and fatal spring. Let the world know that we have invested the Government with the power, for three years to come, of calling every able-bodied man, who has not upon himself the support of a widowed mother, or brothers or sisters of tender age, to the defense of their country. Let them understand that the clergyman is to leave his desk, the laborer the field, the mine, and the workshop, the lawyer his office, and the legislator his seat, and every other man his vocation. Let them know that we have made up our minds, one and all, to march to the defense of justice and liberty, home and country; and that we will, under the Constitution, and by virtue of those powers sneered at as the war power—those rights of a belligerent which superadd themselves to the ordinary functions of the Government whenever it engages in war—maintain the integrity of our Government; that we will, if need be, bring every able-bodied man, irrespective of his color or condition, into the field; and that the foreigner who dares, with unfriendly wish, invade our shores shall die; and they will feel that we will not only conquer the rebellion, but that we offer a fruitless field for intervention.

This is what this bill proposes to do. I care not whether the clause touching "treasonable practices" be in or out of it. I act upon the theory that self-defense inheres in the Government as it does in man, and that those to whom the Government is for the time confided should be empowered to protect it, and are bound to punish all who attempt to do it harm, whether their intent is manifested by action or by the language of conspiracy leading to acts elsewhere. It is the law that one conspirator may be in one State, and another in another, and another in still another State, and all be responsible for the language used by each. No question of jurisdiction arises there. A common intent makes all who have promoted it guilty of the overt act. My judgment is, that where it becomes apparent that a man, with a rebellious heart, and sympathies with those who are in arms against the Government, is by letter or word communicating with or aiding them, he should be dealt with as you deal with a rattlesnake when you hear the rattle near your heel, or as you deal with a copperhead when you perceive its venomous fang approaching your throat. You are not to wait until the sting is in you before you crush the reptile. You must do it while you can save your own life. Herein I charge the Government with having been in default. If the example of our revolutionary sires and of Andrew Jackson had been followed, and some of the men who now clamor and whine about their arbitrary arrests, and tell how their homes were violated, had been tried, allowed five minutes for brief prayer, and then shot or hung, there would have been less treasonable practices, and the Government would have found support where it now receives censure. Therein is my objection to the course of the Administration; and if it were clear that this bill made such conduct on their part necessary, I should vote for it even more joyously than I will to-morrow on its final passage.

THE WAY TO ATTAIN AND SECURE PEACE.

Speech of Hon. W. D. Kelley, of Pennsylvania, delivered in the House of Representatives, December 19, 1862.

Mr. CHAIRMAN, it seems to me that before the week closes some rejoinder should be made to the various suggestions in favor of peace and compromise, and of hostility to the acts and policy of the President of the United States, that we have been hearing from day to day.

Permit me to say, sir, that I am in favor of peace. I was for peace when I first raised my voice in this House. I was then, as I am now, for early and enduring peace—for peace on terms honorable to the people of the country, and which shall not dishonor the memory of the wise and patriotic men who established the independence and unity of our country, and ordained its beneficent institutions.

I am, sir, for peace so secure that it shall prevail forever over that broad territory which, at the last Presidential election, was covered by thirty-four State constitutions, and that which, as territory, belongs to the United States, but which will come under the jurisdiction of States whose people shall know no sovereignty save that which resides in the Constitution as it came to us from the fathers. How, sir, can such a peace be attained? It can only be done by remembering, first and always, that the supreme law of the land is the Constitution of the United States; and that we, as members of this House, are sworn to support that Constitution; and that the President of the United States is sworn to preserve, pro-

tect, and defend it. My theory is, sir, that rights and duties
are things reciprocal. So long as the people of a State obey
the behests of the Constitution, and live in accordance with
them, they are entitled to the enjoyment of all constitutional
rights. So long as they array themselves against them only
in such force that the marshal and his *posse* may suppress
their violent demonstrations, they are entitled to all those
rights, save as the penal code properly applied may abridge
them. But when, as has been the case in the so-called se-
ceding States, they assemble in organic conventions and throw
off all duty to the Government; when they abjure loyalty and
duty, and claim to have established on our soil an independent
and foreign government; when they attempt in the name and
by the agency of such alleged foreign government, to create a
navy, and do assemble armies to contend with the power of
the Government, and thereby banish our customs and postal
system, and close our courts, they lose their title to constitutional rights, and it becomes the duty of the Government, by
whatever f⸳⸳ce it may require, to regain possession and control
of the terri y occupied by them, and to rule the people occupying it with ⸳uch hostile purposes, irrespective of State lines, or
State names, or State institutions, or State constitutions. It
must maintain the unity of the country; and if the inhabitants
will disregard all their duties, it must govern them under the
power of the Constitution that makes the President Commander-in-Chief of the Army and Navy of the United States,
and that requires him, if so it must be, by military force to
maintain the supremacy of the Government over every acre of
our territory. When supreme jurisdiction shall be thus established, we may say to whomsoever may occupy the country, or
particular portions of it, "Adopt your State constitution,
whether the one that formerly prevailed or another; open your
courts, and let the courts of the United States be opened; let
our customs system and our postal system be enforced; avow
your allegiance to our Constitution and Government, and as you
shall perform the duties, enjoy, also, the rights of American
citizens."

Gentlemen on the other side seem to forget that sworn duty,
as well as patriotism and the future welfare and peace of the
country, demand the maintenance of the unity of our territory,
and of the supremacy of the power of the United States over
it in its entirety. These are things that must be maintained,
if we would avoid standing armies and unceasing war. Where

all duties under the Constitution are rejected, no rights can be claimed, and the Government must be maintained by force. That is my position, and it is, I believe, the position of the loyal people of the country. When I say loyal, I mean it; as I know no conditions that may accompany its expression. That loyalty which is conditional stretches forth a friendly hand to treason. Indeed, conditional loyalty is partial treason. The President's emancipation proclamation has been the subject of invective and denunciation this morning, and it has been said that no man in the country, save the President of the United States, believes that it will promote peace. Sir, has territory ceased to be territory? Do figures still indicate numbers and power? Has the lesser come, by some new influence, to comprehend the greater? For, if it be not so, the enforcement of that proclamation will promote peace by aiding in the establishment of the supremacy of the Government. Has not the question as to whether four millions of stalwart people shall labor for us or for those with whom we are at war, some importance, and a direct bearing on the issue? Will its solution, if it transfer them from one side to the other, have no influence upon the power of the rebellion? I believe, with the President, that it will. There are four millions of brawny right arms, mostly dark-colored, but many of them, through the fell influence of the hell-born institution of slavery, fair as our own; there are four millions of people reluctantly giving their daily toil to the support of this rebellion: and it is proposed by the President to invite them, on the 1st of January next, as wisdom would have done more than a year ago, to withhold their labors from that cause, and bestow them, as they desire to, upon the cause of patriotism, freedom, and peace, under the starry flag of our country. Who will tell me that the transfer of the labor of these people will have no influence in suppressing the rebellion?

But, asked the eloquent gentleman from Kentucky, [Mr. YEAMAN,] Who ever heard of a belligerent party taking private property on land? Let me ask him a question: Who ever heard of a belligerent prohibiting the people of the opposing power from rallying to his standard? He speaks of property, and I speak of *men*. It is a great thing, sir, to be a man.

Mr. YEAMAN. I answer the gentleman by saying that slaves, so far from being persons in the eye of the laws of nations, as he treats them, while they are actually persons, are, by that Constitution which he has sworn to support, the private property of private individuals, and that neither under the Constitution, nor under the laws of nations, can you take private property on land as an act of war.

Mr. KELLEY. I take issue with the gentleman there, and if he will say that they are not designated in the Constitution as "persons," or point me to the clause in which they are designated as property, I will yield the point. The Constitution that I have sworn to support tells me that they—yes, the mothers, the fathers and the children all—are "PERSONS held to service." They are persons so held by virtue of that Constitution which has been spurned and trampled and spit upon, and yet he asks that those who have heaped these indignities upon that sacred instrument shall enjoy to the last iota the rights of loyal men under it. Did sane man ever utter so preposterous a proposition before? It is the service of these people we need. The proclamation invites them to our standard. He characterizes them as property. I say, with the Constitution, that they are persons, and as such will welcome them to our support. Their advent to freedom will exclude the necessity of the further draft or conscription of our sons and brothers.

Sir, I was remarking that it is a great thing to be a man, in contrast with horses, cows, and other cattle with which these poor people are habitually classified, and to which they have been assimilated by brutalizing laws. Man chains the lightning, makes the sun his servant, whitens the ocean with sails —his messengers to the poles in quest of knowledge—burdens its great waves with the commodities which his genius and toil have produced and which he is exchanging for others, the products of distant lands, more valuable to him. From the conflicting elements, fire and water, he generates a vapory power that almost annihilates space, and practically removes mountains and levels valleys; and at the close of a life of usefulness, upon the sick-bed, he remembers and reviews the past, cheers, counsels, and blesses those about him, and, looking to heaven, feels that with God he is to live forever. The gentleman looks upon these millions of persons as property—so do bad institutions pervert gentle and generous natures. I say, sir, they are capable of all that ennobles man, and all that endears woman to man, and all that opens to either the great hereafter and its blessed hopes. It is of these women, these children, these men, I speak, and I say that he can point to no case in which a belligerent has refused the aid of such as these when engaged in a war such as that which now engrosses and exhausts the energies of this country. Sir, the only thing about the President's proclamation that struck me as amiss was, that it was not, like the lightning, to take instant effect, and that its beneficent result should be postponed to so distant a day. Are these people or the relation in which they stand to those who hold them to service, like cotton, leather, railroad depots, bad whisky, and other supposed analogous things suggested by the gentleman from Kentucky, yesterday? No, no. Trace back the laws of war, so elaborately described by the gentleman from Maryland [Mr. CRISFIELD] to-day, and you will find that the invading force not only has always welcomed acquisitions from the ranks of the enemy, but that, in the good old days of chivalry, a herald invariably proceeded to the gates of a besieged town and offered immunity and protection to all who would join the invading power. This chivalric example the President's proclamation pledges him to follow on the coming in of the glad new year. Let us hail the auspicious day!

I come back to the question with which I started. Will the gentleman from Maryland, [Mr. CRISFIELD,] will the gentleman from Kentucky, [Mr. YEAMAN,] will the gentleman from Illinois, [Mr. RICHARDSON,] will any one of these gentlemen, or of their learned coadjutors, say that it is not the duty of the President to maintain the unity of the country and the supremacy of the Constitution over all our territory? And if they will not say that, is there one of them who will say that he was wrong in thus inviting four millions of the people of the country to abandon rebellion and rally to the standard of loyalty, peace, and the Constitution? No one of them, I apprehend, will say so. Than this, in my judgment, mere sympathy with the rebellion could no further go. Gentlemen deny that slavery was the cause of this war. Let me ask them which one of the non-slaveholding States, from the first, has proposed to participate in it, and which one of the slaveholding States has been free from a desire to participate in it, or from overt acts of rebellion? Why is it that prevailing loyalty and treason find their boundaries just here, if slavery be not the controlling influence? I give praise to the Border States for all they have done on the side of the country; but I remember that the first of the troops from my State to find service found it in the lower part of little Delaware; I remember that Marylanders were the first to shed the blood of New England in this unholy war; I remember that it is but recently, if indeed the question be at all settled, that Kentucky has been able to say with assurance that she has given more soldiers to the Union than to the rebel army.

All honor and glory to the men of East Tennessee. The heroic devotion to the Constitution they have exhibited, and the barbarous cruelties they have endured, make a chapter which even the people of the Southern States will, long years hence, dwell on, perhaps with mingled pride and pain, but with more interest than on any other in American history. We know how terribly that State has been ravaged by the prevalence of the rebellion within its limits. And Missouri, which has not only elected unconditional loyalists, but unconditional emancipationists to this House, has also been the bloody battle-field in which Missourians have been engaged in either army. If it be not true, sir, that slavery is the root of this rebellion, I ask some inspired man to indicate its moving cause, for human wisdom cannot detect it elsewhere.

Now, can it be possible, Mr. Chairman, that the only right so secured on earth that men cannot abjure it, nor government divest them of it, even to save itself in death struggle, is the right of holding fellow-beings in bondage? The proposition that we have not the right to invite these slaves to freedom and our standard involves just this theory—that the rebels cannot by the most flagrant treason divest themselves of the right to hold these people in bondage; that the people cannot acquire freedom for themselves, and that no power in the Constitution, or in the war power, or deducible from history or philosophy, can relieve them from the duty of assisting the enemies of the country to destroy its life. Let the arguments be expressed as they may, with all the eloquence and elegance with which care and time have clothed them in the mouths of the gentlemen from Kentucky and Maryland, [Messrs. YEAMAN and CRISFIELD,] they come to this. And until gentlemen can demonstrate this extraordinary proposition, they cannot impair the force of the President's proclamation, in accordance, as it is, with all law and all history, with the best impulses of humanity, and the spirit of our charter of freedom, and with the growing tendency of our age. The gentleman from Maryland asks, "will this bring peace? Will the South ever consent to come in under such an arrangement?" Sir, I do not propose to, nor ought the Government to ask the South on what terms it will come in. What the Government ought to do, and what I trust it will do, is to go straight forward and establish its power by crushing out all armed resistance, and when that is done, let it govern the region as a Territory, if the people will not establish their own government. In this condition let the contumacious remain; but whenever they will establish governments for themselves, adopt State constitutions, open the courts, elect Legislatures, and by them and the people elect Senators and members of Congress, receive them as States into the Union, under such designations as they may choose, whether novel or familiar. By this means, the forms and vital principles of our Government will be preserved, and peace and constitutional freedom be secured to the people of distant ages. Whenever this Government puts forth its power to the end that it is bound to assert, there will be no question as to whether we mean to violate the Constitution or whether the people of the South will accept the constitutional terms we offer them.

"But," said the gentleman this morning, "will the Border States tolerate it?" To be sure they will. True, many of their citizens may dislike to see the Southern market closed against their human cattle; but the rebellion has gone so far that, with the 1st of January, slavery dies south of the Border State line; and when there is no market for men, women, and children, south of Virginia and Kentucky, slavery will have small value in any of the Border States. I think I see the hand of God in these movements. The events of the times are deplorable, indeed; but I know that His providences are inscrutable, and that He can make the folly and wrath of man to praise Him. I had long seen that if the Democratic party could continue the misrule which it had enforced on the people for years, and especially its aggressions upon the rights of the laborers of the country, a war would come which would be at the door of every man's home. Let us look at it. "A house divided against itself cannot stand," quoted my friend from Maryland, and with grave deprecation. Did not the leaders of the South divide our house? Let us look at it. Go where you will, Mr. Chairman, in our Northern States, you find the Constitution of the United States taught in our elementary schools, and its democratic spirit everywhere inculcated. You find our youth growing up at the foot of the hustings; and the great doctrine taught to every child is: "You are as good as any other child. When you come to manhood you are to be equal, before the State, of every other man. You must watch, guard, and maintain all your rights."

Thus is the democratic sentiment stimulated in every school, from every lecture stand, at every political gathering; and the political sentiment of the whole North is that of individualism and equality. And once in seven days comes the Sabbath; and from hillside and valley, from the lanes and alleys, as well as from the broad streets of the city, the children gather in the church and Sunday-School: there they learn that Christianity enforces while it refines and exalts the doctrines inculcated in the secular school; thus the religious sentiment adds its great power to the political. "These poor are as good as you," says the teacher. "These blind, and lame, and halt, are the children of your Father; and inasmuch as you do kindness unto them, you perform your duty unto Him." Thus the political and religious sentiments blend; and theirs is an ever-growing power. Of this we have ample evidence all over the North, in the elaborate comforts of our eleemosynary institutions, and the care that is taken of our prisoners. The deaf, the dumb, the blind, the insane, are cared for. Homes are established for friendless children, where the waifs of society, the offspring of the destitute and fallen, the pauper and the felon, are cared for and reared in these teachings of democracy and Christianity. Thus the sentiment spreads and deepens and grows.

We have one institution in the North, the outgrowth of the perpetual contest between labor and capital, that, could the South have carried its domination a little further, would have made war and bloodshed over the whole country. It consists of hardy working men, and is known as the trades' union. We at the North live by wages. Our men are familiar with toil; our women do not shrink from it. We recognize the maxim, as true to-day as the day when it was first written in homely English :—

> "Man labors from sun to sun,
> But woman's work is never done."

We all labor, and wages is the foundation of the welfare and abundance of our people. The idea that induced this rebellion and the supremacy of which could alone have averted it, was that slavery should be not only extended into the new Territories of the country, but be domesticated in all the States. It was first to be introduced into the States by gentlemen *in transitu* with their colonies. The roll of Mr. Toombs's slaves was to be called at the foot of Bunker Hill. We were told in social in-

tercourse in Philadelphia, of Mr. Yancey, that he would yet
visit Independence Hall with his slaves. The re-establi.hment
of the right to hold slaves all over the country was the purpose
of the leaders of our "wayward sisters." Nothing less would
satisfy them. Sir, had that thing been accomplished, the
trade unions of the North would either have throttled the
slaveholders, or, under the influence of the prejudices of caste
and color, throttled the unhappy slaves—perhaps both. Here
let me notice the remark of the gentleman from Maryland,
that he does not agree with either of the two factions. Of
what factions does he speak? The Governments of the Union
and the Confederacy? Sir, it is the first time I ever heard the
Government of the United States denounced as a faction in
the Halls of Congress. Nor are they who are devot'ng all
their energies to the support of the President and the Constitution to be denounced as a faction. I look in vain through
this House for two factions.

I see that the Government, with a million of men, defending
itself and attempting to enforce its laws over its own dom'nions,
has been resisted by a body of armed rebels, and that those
who sympathize with them, in a greater or less degree, are
attempting to embarrass it; but other faction I have not been
able to discover. There were two factions before the war
broke out. Anterior to that event, there was a body of men
in the North, who, under Christian impulses, believing it to be
a duty to labor for the oppressed, and that it is a crime to hold
men and women in bondage, were willing to violate all civic
restraints in order to give freedom, culture, and hope to the
slave. The Abolitionists may have been entitled to that epi-
thet. And there were Southern men, on the other hand, determined, as I have indicated, to carry their institutions all
over the North—to make slavery national by perverting the
Constitution. There were, then, two factions—devotion to
right and justice, perhaps not restrained by a proper prudence
on the one hand; and love of lucre, power, and lust, that
blotted out all sympathy with humanity, on the other, charac-
terized the leaders of these factions.

Had the Southern faction been permitted to dominate until
the roll of Southern slaves had been called in every county in
every Northern State, there would have broken out a war—a
war coextensive with the country, and bloody, at every
hearthstone—a war which might have been of races, or in
which those who claimed their human property would have

suffered with their unhappy and proscribed chattels. The white men of the North, who, from their own hard-earned and hoarded wages, will support their unemployed craftsman rather than let him work for under wages, would hardly have permitted men to work beside them for nothing, and throw their babies as property into the scale with their unrequited toil.

Sir, I believe this war was inevitable. The insane ambition and mad, craving lust of the South could be checked alone by the results of war. It had closed its ears hermetically against the voice of persuasion and reason. And wherever slavery existed that ambition and that lust had root. Slavery did cause this war. It was destined to cause war, and if not put in process of eradication, will involve our posterity in war. Is it not fitting, therefore, that the result of the war shall be the end of slavery? The President's proclamation does not propose to touch the institution in the Border States. But, as I have said, with the market for the annual crop gone, it will be found to be of no more value in Kentucky than it is now found to be in Missouri, with her free surroundings. And then we will come to what I am prepared to say very few words upon, the compensated emancipation proposition of the President.

The countless millions, the millions of millions that we have heard from the other side are to be expended in compensated emancipation, will be somewhat reduced when we come to remember that it is only the loyal men of the Border States that we will have to deal with.

Missouri is here, asking $10,000,000 on condition that she emancipates her slaves within a little more than a year. In God's name, let us give it to her; and if Kentucky and Maryland make the same claim, let us give it to them, and pay our full share out of the results of our own hard labor at the North. Let us even, by an addition to our already grievous burden of taxes imposed by this war—slavery's own offspring —share the losses of those whose slaves shall be exalted into freemen.

But, say the gentlemen, the proclamation is unconstitutional and illegal, and therefore void. I fear self-interest blinds some of them. It is a professional maxim that he has a fool for a client who takes charge of his own case. Certainly, no disinterested lawyer will dispute the validity of the proclamation of the commander-in-chief inviting to our flag people of the rebel States, and promising them protection and the enjoyment of constitutional rights. But will the proclamation be enforced?

Yes, that is certain as the coming of the new year. And I ask the gentleman from Kentucky [Mr. YEAMAN] and the gentleman from Maryland [Mr. CRISFIELD] to pause in the career they open by their speeches of yesterday and to-day. Both profess, truly I doubt not, to desire peace; both assure us that they would give utterance to no words that would add to the discord of the country. Let them then look the facts in the face. Gentlemen, do you not see that time and Providence are conspiring with man to put an end to the sole source of discord to the country? Do you not see that it was this institution which created division even in the convention that formed our Constitution? Do you not see that it has been this institution that, from the early settlement of the country down to the present time, has produced more of discord than all other causes combined?

The eloquent gentleman from Kentucky yesterday asserted that this rebellion had been ripening from 1798. I agree with him that that was one stand-point in its progress. The resolutions of 1798 marked a new epoch. But if he will go further back, he will find, in the debates of the convention which framed the Constitution, abundant evidence that slavery was and had been a source of discord, and that it came well-nigh preventing the establishment of a Union. It has been a source of discord only; never was it a blessing to any State or people.

I have no special love for the negro. I am proud of the race of which, by the blessing of God, I am a member. It is not for the negro that I plead. The gentleman from Illinois [Mr. RICHARDSON] the other day said that all our sympathy and all our action was for the negro, but not one thing did we propose to do for the white man. Has he never heard of the creature—MAN? I speak for man, the child of God, irrespective of the color of his skin.

Look at the baneful influence of slavery upon both white and black. You point me to statistics from the North to show that poverty and crime prevail with the negro there in undue proportion. I point you back to your laws that made it a felony to teach him to read and write, by which he might have drawn moral precepts and power from the same sources that your white children draw them. I point back to the fact that you have never allowed him the stimulus of hope. I say that your accursed institution, and the cruelty and depression inseparable from it, have not only filled our jails with your victims, but has brought poverty to both races wherever it has

borne with assurance that it was hers even through childhood. It is this which has made you poor, notwithstanding your mineral deposits, your rivers, and your vast agricultural resources. You have made the negro a curse to you; for God never permits a great wrong to go unpunished.

When, in another year, Congress assembles in these halls, there will be no pictures drawn such as the gentlemen have furnished us with, of homes desolated or destroyed, women ravished, masters murdered by slaves converted into freemen and grateful for the greatest blessing of life. The voice of thanksgiving and praise will come from every heart to whom freedom has been given. It will come from the white man as well as the freed slaves, in tones of praise and hallelujah.

There is, however, one thing the people of the rebellious States have to guard against. Of that they must beware. Let them not undertake to re-enslave the freed men that the President of the United States delivers by his proclamation, or woe may betide them. Let them not thus invite the horrors of St. Domingo. The voice of history admonishes them fully on this point. If they do, it will be their act, and not the President's or ours. He will make them free, and they will rejoice in their freedom and be humbly grateful. Not in the hour of joy and gratitude, and when singing praises for their deliverance, is the tiger let loose in men. As God will have wrought this change, He will guide it. But let man attempt to reverse His providence, and who shall answer for his folly?

REMARKS OF MR. KELLEY, OF PENNSYLVANIA, ON ARMING THE NEGROES.

Delivered in the House of Representatives, January, 1863.

SIR, this is, in my judgment, a humane and wise provision for hastening the settlement of the war now pending; but gentlemen on the other side find in it an instigation to servile insurrection, the degradation of our army, and a blot upon our legislation and history, which no future glories can wipe out. The distinguished gentleman from Kentucky, who first addressed us to-day, [Mr. WICKLIFFE,] denounces Hunter's colored regiment as a failure. From whom did he hear that the first regiment of South Carolina volunteers have proved to be a failure? I know General Hunter to be a man of veracity, and the mails by the last steamer from the South tell us that he addressed that regiment less than a week ago, saying, among other things—

"I am glad to be in the midst of you, glad to have seen so fine an exhibition of proficiency as you have shown this day. I only wish I had a hundred thousand of you to fight for the freedom of the Union."

He said further—and he has had nearly a year of observation, and is a man familiar with military history—

"I see no reason why you should not make as good soldiers as any in the world, and I trust that upon all occasions you will be found willing to do your whole duty."

The gentlemen from Illinois, Indiana, and Ohio have told us of the courage and endurance exhibited by colored soldiers and sailors in the earlier wars of the country, and on several occasions in this. May I not remind you that it is now, sir, just a year since I had the honor of calling the attention of the House to an extract from a letter from Commodore Dupont? It was when the country was still thrilling with the glory of the naval action at Port Royal. I read from that letter the expression of his gratitude to the "contrabands" who rallied around him, and his declaration that—

"They serve us with zeal, make no bargains for their remuneration, go under fire without the slightest hesitation; and, indeed, in our cause are as 'insensible to fear' as Governor Pickens. Some of them are very intelligent."

But, asks the venerable gentleman from Kentucky, who last addressed us, [Mr. CRITTENDEN,] what is the reason for wanting these colored men? This is the reason. It is not only the duty of the President to maintain the supremacy of the power of the United States over all its territory, but, sir, it is part of the providence of God that that supremacy should be maintained. You find that providence written in the topography of the country; you find it in the institutions of the country; you find it in our national progress and development. Look with the eye of the philosopher or statesman over the surface of our grand country; scan the lay of its mountains, the courses of its rivers, or search our history, and everywhere you will find it written by the hand of God that the territory now occupied by the United States was destined from the beginning for the home of one people, to be presided over by one government. It is necessary that this government be maintained in this crisis; and it is not fair, to say the least, that, in a war the results of which are to bless both North and South—a war which, if well fought out, is to bless the generations that shall dwell through all time in this vast country of ours, all the hardships and privations should be borne by the people of the Northern States alone. This bill authorizes the President of the United States to call upon the people occupying the territory in rebellion for their quota of the army. And why shall they not yield it? Why shall not all that territory send as fair a percentage of its people to war for the Union as the State of Rhode Island, or its neighbor of grander dimensions, New York? Will the gentleman answer that question? Where are the South Carolinians rallying under the Union flag; the Georgians, the Mississipians, the men of any of the eleven States in rebellion? And does he mean to say that the stain and infamy of this rebellion shall forever attach to the South— that it shall not be wiped out by the loyal men of that section? God forbid it! We never could dwell together as brethren again were it not that we mean to let the men of the South do their share in restoring their own government. Let the loyal men of the South take a full part in this war, and subjugation will be deprived of its power to embitter the future of the nation. The North cannot indulge in the exultation of conquerors if she shall but have assisted the loyal men of the South to maintain a common blessing.

Sir, there is philosophic and patriotic reason why the President should bring from all these whilom States their fair quota of the army of freedom and the Constitution. But let me, waiving these for the time, consider some simple questions. Why should it not be done? Is the life of the negro more sacred than that of the white man? Why should not American Africans encounter the power of the enemy and the malaria of the swamps? Why should your son, and my brother, and our friends die that the negro may live? I do not esteem him one whit better than ourselves; nor do I deny that he is our equal in rights before the great God our common Father, and in the great forum where absolute justice prevails. I assert that he is not better than we, and should share the dangers and sufferings of this war. I ask, again, is it more essential to the slave's wife or to the free colored man's that he should protect and shelter her, to his children, that he should watch over them, than it is to the white wife and children of the loyal States that they should enjoy the care and affection of husband and father; and is it upon this assumption that Democrats and gentlemen from the Border States will not allow his sacred person to encounter the risks of the deck of a man-of-war, or of storming the breastwork or the battery? If this reason influences them it is a new-found faith. They have at least not shown devotion to it in the past. If one of them wanted to give a dinner-party, and had not ready cash, under the laws and civilization which have moulded their sentiments, he could put a wife and mother upon the auction block, and leave her children orphaned for all time, and her husband to pine for the one being that he loved. No, the slave is only important to his wife and child as the thing around which their affections cling. He is alike powerless to protect her or provide nurture for them: but our Northern laboring man is the head of a family and home; it is upon his labor that his wife depends to make the home comfortable and cheerful, and it is by the aid of his labor that the humble boy is to climb the hill from poverty to wealth, from ignorance to learning, from obscurity, it may be, to fame. Why, then, shall not the black man leave wife and child for this war as well as the white man?

Or do gentlemen strive to defeat this bill because they deem it important that the rebels shall have a more adequate supply of labor than we? They all know that every white company recruited takes our laborers from the field, the mine, the workshop. Do they not know that our power at home is impaired in the ratio of the power and consistency of the regiment or division? Has not their whole policy been to deprive us of labor, of strength at home, of character, and to secure to our enemies a supply of labor to maintain them, while they cut our throats, and rob the graves of our soldiers that they may make trinkets for ladies' girdles of their bones? Let the laborers of the rebels strike for freedom, not in lawless insurrection, but under the guidance of officers who receive their orders from the Executive mansion of the United States. But, says the venerable gentleman from Kentucky, [Mr. CRITTENDEN,] even Catiline refused to employ slaves in war. Catiline, sir, was a bad man, a base man, a rebel and conspirator; but how infinitely glorious he stands beside the leaders of this rebellion, if the gentleman's statements and impressions be correct, for they have done from the start, what he tells us Catiline was not base enough to do, brought their slaves into the field against their brethren! I have been calling them Catilines. I beg pardon of the shade of Catiline for associating his name with those of villains of so much deeper dye.

The gentleman smoothly commenced by saying, "it is true, that gentlemen, by sedulously studying history, have discovered a few cases in which the negro has served faithfully in military matters." By sedulously studying history? Has the gentleman ever heard that there is an empire called British India? If he has, I tell him that a race blacker than the children of our rebel brethren, black as the stock from which they got them, won for England British India. Does the gentleman's historical reading all antedate this century? Does he not know that in the last glories which crowned the valor of European arms, the Turcos were honored by all their companions for the skill and reckless courage with which they led

3

every forlorn hope? and these Turcos had not enjoyed for two hundred years the *christianizing influence* of American slavery. They were the fresh material of which our slaves of lighter hue are partially made. Where, let me, as the champion in this contest of a down-trodden race, ask him—and I will give him the remainder of the session to answer—have arms ever been placed in their hands, and they brought fairly into the field, and failed the power which relied upon them? I ask for a single case. One of the earliest play-grounds of my childhood was a spot in Jersey—not the State of my nativity, but of my paternal ancestors—called Red Bank; and, as I learned at the knees of others the history of my country, and what made that spot sacred, perhaps a little of what the gentleman calls abolition was infused into me, for there I learned that when Donop was pursuing the broken American forces, a black battalion stepped in and redeemed the fortunes of the day. I think that battalion, Mr. Speaker, was led by a citizen of your State, Rhode Island. Where, I ask, in our history or any other, has the down-trodden race failed on the battle-field to show that it has been its affectionate humanity that has kept its terrific courage in check through centuries of wrong and oppression?

But the gentleman asks, will you turn loose this terrible population to make insurrection? No, sir. I would not withdraw from that race the promised word of hope. I would not do with them, since the President's proclamation has been made known to them, what the French undertook to do in St. Domingo. I would not, after having quickened their pulses by the word "freedom," and taught them to gaze at hope's star with tearless eye, madden them by saying, "You are slaves again, and incapable of being free. You must win by indiscriminate slaughter your freedom, or remain in slavery forever." I would bring the loyal men of South Carolina, North Carolina, Texas, and every rebellious State, however black they may be, under the flag of the nation, and under military discipline. I would give them wages, and train them to the habits of freemen; and while they cement with their blood, and raise anew by their courage, the great temple of American freedom, our women will care for their women and benighted children, and carry to them that truth so mighty to us, that there is a God, and that they, too, are the subjects of redeeming grace. Our women in the North never see poverty, ignorance, or suffering, which they do not strive to mitigate and soothe; and, by the end of the five years, which the gentleman from Kentucky thinks so horrible a period, there will be developed a race of negroes who will know that there are figures and letters and words, and will know, too, what few of them do in any fair sense, that there is for them hope and prosperity in this world, and immortality beyond the grave.

I fear not a standing army of a particular color. I fear a standing army. I tell the gentleman that this country was not made for a particular generation, or for a particular number of the members of a generation. It was made for those who shall occupy it through all time; and if Eli Thayer can lead five thousand free Germans into Florida, in God's name let him take them there. The gentleman [Mr. WICKLIFFE] said they would starve there, and he pictured it as a land of stone and swamp, if I heard him right. I have deemed it one of the fairest lands in God's world. But, sir, be it all that he describes it, let white labor go there, and make the black laborer on the soil free, and you will find it to bloom and bear as rocky Massachusetts does. If it be all that the gentleman describes it, free labor will there vindicate the truth of the maxim that "plant slavery in a garden, and it will become a desert; plant free labor in a desert, and it will become a garden." Let them go and settle the country. The great object of this war, as I have said, is to maintain the life of the nation, and to give to the people of the future those beneficent institutions which, in eighty years, have made us the first power in the world physically, and given us of the free States a civilization trascendently above the highest known elsewhere: to save these institutions and this system, and to perpetuate them so long as God reigns, and man lives on earth. If we do but fight out this war safely, we will secure to all the millions, the hundreds, nay, probably the thousands of millions who shall dwell here, peace, liberty, hope, and the results of these.

Sir, I am but a poor and feeble civilian. I have done little duty of a military character in my life. But this glimpse at the future grandeur of my country recalls one night of military duty to my memory. I had the honor, Mr. Speaker, of being an humble member of that great body of the people of Pennsylvania who rushed to the southern frontier of Western Maryland, to protect the boundary of their own State, and, as it proved, the flank of that great and gallant army which was then supposed to have won a decisive victory at Antietam. It may not be generally known that the militia of Pennsylvania protected the flank of that army from Friday noon till Sunday at eleven o'clock. It was during that time that I lay down one night, carbine in hand, and gazed at the Milky Way with its innumerable myriads of stars; and while I thought of home and family, and of the apparent folly of a man who, until then, had scarcely known how to handle the weapon he held, rushing to such a post, I also thought of the grandeur of my country, and of its immense future. I felt, sir, that in this great struggle the life of the best-loved or greatest of us all, or the sorrow of families, was no more in comparison with the cause than was the smallest star in all that immense multitude to the sum of the material universe. And I have felt since that hour that to secure the peace and unity of the country I would sacrifice the lives of the grandest and most delicate by thousands, and of the powerful and muscular and least valuable by tens of thousands. We must secure peace by achieving supremacy at whatever cost. But let not the North be asked to do it all. Authorize the President to call upon the rebellious territory to furnish its fair quota. Arm, equip, and pay those who respond to his call. And when you have done so, the rebellion will end. These gentlemen will no longer be able to serve the rebellion by protecting the laborers of rebels, and thus furnishing them

with men to handle their cannon, dig their trenches, grow
their food, make their clothes, and serve—as the record shows
they have served throughout the war—in fighting their battles.
Let gentlemen show the country, if they can, that it is better
negroes should shoot loyal men than traitors; and when they
have done so, let them take out a patent for their own loyalty.

LETTER FROM SECRETARY CHASE.

WASHINGTON, April 9. 1863.

GENTLEMEN: Imperative demands on my time compel me to
deny myself the gratification of attending the meeting to which
you kindly invite me.

You will meet to send words of cheer to our brave generals
and soldiers in the field, to rebuke treason in our midst, giving, in the garb of peace, aid and comfort to treason in the
panoply of war, to maintain inviolate the integrity of the national territory and the supremacy of the national Constitution
and laws, to strengthen the hands and nerve the heart of the
President for the great work to which God and the people have
called him. For what other purpose can American citizens
now assemble?

It is my fixed faith, gentlemen, that God does not mean
that this American Republic shall perish. We are tried as by
fire, but our country will live. Notwithstanding all the vio-
lence and the machinations of traitors and their sympathizers,
on this or the other side of the Atlantic, our country will
live.

And while our country lives, slavery, the chief source, and
cause, and agent of our ills, will die. The friends of the Union
in the South, before the rebellion, predicted the destruction of
slavery as a consequence of secession. if that madness should
prevail. Nothing, in my judgment, is more certain than the
fulfillment of these predictions. Safe in the States before re-

bellion, from all Federal interference, slavery has come out from its shelter under State Constitutions and laws to assail the national life. It will surely die, pierced by its own fangs and stings.

What matter, now, how it dies? Whether as a consequence or object of the war, what matter? Is this a time to split hairs of logic? To me it seems that Providence indicates clearly enough how the end of slavery must come. It comes in rebel Slave States by military order, decree, or proclamation, not to be disregarded or set aside, in any event, as a nullity, but maintained and executed with perfect good faith to all the enfranchised, and it will come in loyal Slave States by the unconstrained action of the people and their legislators, aided freely and generously by their brethren of the Free States. I may be mistaken in this, but if I am, another better way will be revealed.

Meantime, it seems to me very necessary to say distinctly, what many yet shrink from saying. The American blacks must be called into this conflict, not as cattle, not now, even as contrabands, but as men. In the Free States and by the proclamation, in the rebel States, they are free men. The Attorney-General, in an opinion which defies refutation, has pronounced these freedmen citizens of the United States. Let then the example of Andrew Jackson, who did not hesitate to oppose colored regiments to British invasion, be now fearlessly followed. Let those blacks, acclimated, familiar with the country, capable of great endurance, receive suitable military organization, and do their part. We need their good-will, and must make them our friends; we must have them for guides, for scouts, for all military service in camp or field for which they are qualified. Thus employed, from a burden, they will become a support, and the hazards, privations, and labors of the white soldiers will be proportionably diminished.

Some one will object, of course. There are always objectors to everything practical. Let experience dispel honest fears, and refute captious or disloyal cavil.

Above all, gentlemen, let no doubt rest on our resolution to sustain, with all our hearts, and with all our means, the soldiers now in arms for the Republic. Let their ranks be filled up; let their supplies be sufficient and regular; let their pay be sure. Let nothing be wanting to them which can insure activity and efficiency. Let each brave officer and man realize that his country's love attends him, and that his country's hopes hang on him, and, inspired by this thought, let him dare and do all that is possible to be dared and done.

So, gentlemen, with the blessing of God, we will make a glorious future. I see it rising before me—how beautiful and grand! There is not time to speak of it now: but from all quarters of the land comes the voice of the sovereign people rebuking faction, denouncing treason, and proclaiming the indivisible unity of the Republic, and in the Heaven-inspired union of the people for the sake of the Union is the sure promise of that splendid hereafter.

With great respect, yours very truly,

S. P. CHASE.

www.ingramcontent.com/pod-product-compliance
Lightning Source LLC
Chambersburg PA
CBHW021604270326
41931CB00009B/1362